My
Favorite
Dogs

GERMAN SHEPHERD

Jinny Johnson

A⁺

Smart Apple Media

Published by Smart Apple Media
P.O. Box 1329
Mankato, MN 56002

Printed in the United States of America,
at Corporate Graphics in North Mankato, Minnesota.

Designed by Hel James
Edited by Mary-Jane Wilkins

Library of Congress Cataloging-in-Publication Data

Johnson, Jinny, 1949-
German shepherd / by Jinny Johnson.
    p. cm. -- (My favorite dogs)
Includes index.
 Summary: "Describes the care, training, and rearing of the German shepherd. Also
explains the German shepherd's unique characteristics and history"--Provided by
publisher.
 ISBN 978-1-59920-842-8 (hardcover, library bound)
 1. German shepherd dog--Juvenile literature. I. Title.
 SF429.G37J64 2013
 636.737'6--dc23
                            2012012144

Photo acknowledgements t = top, b = bottom
page 1 Ron Rowan Photography/Shutterstock; 3 iStockphoto/Thinkstock;
4-5 Nikolai Tsvetkov/Shutterstock; 6 Mikel Martinez/Shutterstock;
7 iStockphoto/Thinkstock; 8-9 iStockphoto/Thinkstock; 10 Oliver Hoffmann/
Shutterstock; 11 Liliya Kulianionak/Shutterstock; 12 Fesus Robert/Shutterstock;
13t remik44992/Shutterstock, b Erik Lam/Shutterstock; 14 iStockphoto/
Thinkstock; 15 s-eyerkaufer/Shutterstock; 16 deepspacedave/Shutterstock;
17 Kachalkina Veronika/Shutterstock; 18 Julien/Shutterstock; 19 Mikel Martinez/
Shutterstock; 20 Monika Wisniewska/Shutterstock; 21 AlexKZ/Shutterstock;
22 Monika Wisniewska/Shutterstock; 23 Lukrecja/Shutterstock
Cover Eric Isselée/Shutterstock

DAD0504
042012
9 8 7 6 5 4 3 2 1

Contents

I'm a German Shepherd!

I'm a faithful, loving companion and once I get to know you, I'll always be your friend.

I'm brave and strong, too. I can be a good guard dog if I'm properly trained.

What I Need

I'm a big, active dog so I need
to be kept busy. I like
to take a good long
walk every day and
I enjoy running and
fetching a ball too.

I love to be around people.
Don't leave me on my own
for too long or I will
be unhappy and
bark a lot.

The German Shepherd

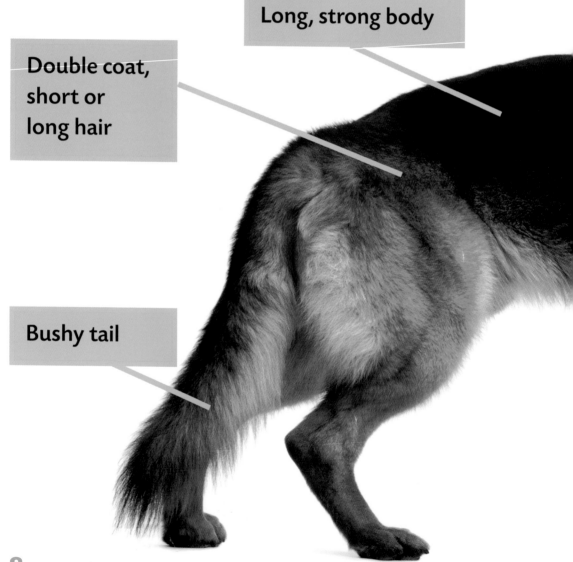

Long, strong body

Double coat,
short or
long hair

Bushy tail

Slightly pointed ears, held upright

Dark eyes

Long muzzle

Black nose

Height: 22–26 inches
(56–66 cm)

Weight: 77–85 pounds
(35–38 kg)

Color: Range of colors
including black, black
and tan, and sable
(multi-colored hairs
with black tips)

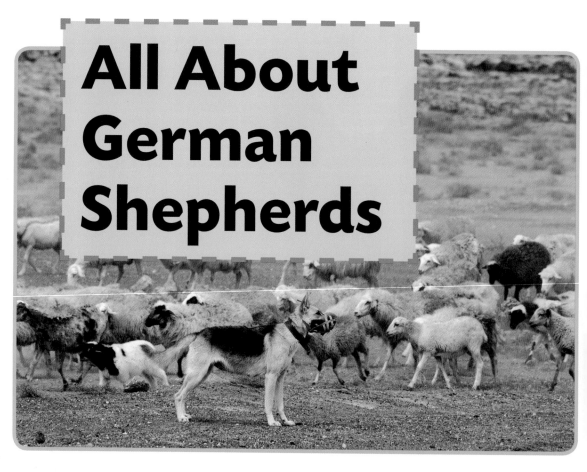

All About German Shepherds

A German soldier first bred German shepherd dogs more than 100 years ago.

The dogs worked herding sheep and they are still used for herding.

The most famous German shepherd was Rin Tin Tin, who took part in more than 26 movies. He also had his own radio show.

Now German shepherds are one of the most popular breeds of dog in the United States.

Growing Up

German shepherd pups need to be with their mom until they are about eight weeks old.

When you first take your puppy home he may miss his family, so be very kind and gentle. Make sure you keep him company,

as he may get anxious when left by himself. German shepherd puppies love to chew, so give him lots of safe toys and chews.

Training Your Dog

German shepherds are very intelligent, but they need to be carefully trained and shown who is boss. The dog should learn to see his owner as his pack leader.

If badly trained, a German shepherd can become aggressive and may bite.

It's a good idea to get your puppy used to lots of different people and places while he is young.

Helping People

German shepherds are brave dogs and are used by the military and for search and rescue work. Search and rescue dogs can help to find people after accidents such as avalanches or explosions.

A German shepherd dog being trained for military work.

German shepherds have a very good sense of smell and can be trained to sniff out gas leaks and other dangers.

Police Dogs

German shepherds are excellent police dogs. They are alert, trustworthy, and intelligent and not immediately friendly to strangers. They can be trained to chase and capture, as well as for crowd control.

Agility training,
when dogs
practice dealing
with obstacles, is an important
part of a police dog's education.

Your Healthy German Shepherd

Brush your dog every day, as German shepherds shed lots of hair.

Bathing a German shepherd can dry out his skin so only give your dog a bath if he gets really dirty. Check his ears every week and call the vet if there are any signs of infection. Gently clean any dirt from the ears.

German shepherds can have hip and elbow problems, so have a puppy checked out before buying.

Caring for Your Dog

You and your family must think very carefully before buying a German shepherd. Remember, he may live for

at least ten years and need lots of attention.

Every day your dog will need food, water, and exercise, as

well as lots of love and care. He will also need to go to the vet for regular checks and vaccinations. When you and your family go out or away on vacation, you will have to make plans for your dog to be looked after.

Useful Words

avalanche
A huge amount of snow that suddenly slides down a mountainside.

muzzle
The long face of an animal such as a dog.

vaccinations
Injections given by the vet to protect your dog against certain illnesses.

Index